MEDITATION FOR BEGINNERS

How to Relieve Stress, Anxiety and Depression and Return to a State of Inner Peace and Happiness

Yesenia Chavan

Evita Publishing, PO Box 306, Station A, Vancouver Island, BC V9W 5B1 Canada

Table of Contents

Introduction

Thank you for purchasing my book *Meditation for Beginners: How to Relieve Stress, Anxiety and Depression and Return to a State of Inner Peace and Happiness*. Also, congratulations about being proactive about applying the life-changing benefits of meditation to your life.

With *Meditation for Beginners* you're going to learn exactly how to meditate, how to use meditation techniques to calm your mind and how to practice meditation daily.

Learning how to meditate and developing a regular meditation practice doesn't have to be difficult. Yes, meditation can seem difficult at first and learning how to take control of your mind can be a challenge, but meditating for only a few minutes a day can help you significantly reduce stress, improve your physical and mental health, maximize your ability to focus and increase productivity.

Buddhism teaches that taking control of your mind through meditation is the only real antidote to stress, anxiety and depression. Scientific studies have validated this and offer proof that meditation CAN in fact change brain chemistry and alter brain waves.

If your meditation efforts have been frustrating, don't worry. *Meditation for Beginners* will help you overcome the common obstacles to developing a long term meditation habit.

Meditation is simply a skill that you need to develop. It's like riding a bike. Yes, you fall at first but eventually your ability to meditate becomes no problem and your meditation practice becomes the most enjoyable, most refreshing and life-giving part of your day.

People who meditate regularly experience less worry, anxiety and stress and are more positive, happy, healthy, productive and successful.

You too can experience the amazing life-changing benefits of meditation by patiently implementing the principles outlined in this book today!

Chapter 1

What is Meditation?

Meditation is the dissolution of thoughts in Eternal awareness or Pure consciousness without objectification, knowing without thinking, merging finitude in infinity.
- Voltaire

In order to understand what meditation is, it is first necessary to look at life from the standpoint of what we as human beings can control. Do we have complete control over every aspect of our lives or is our control limited?

At first you might be tempted to say that you do have complete control over every aspect of your life, but when you dig a little deeper you will find that the only two things that you can *completely* control in life are your thoughts and actions. That's it. Most things are simply beyond your control.

Fortunately, the power to take responsibility for your personal state of mind *is* something you have control over. Therefore, you have the ability to change your state of mind for the better.

According to Buddhism this is an important thing that you can and should do for yourself. In fact, Buddhism believes that taking complete control of your state of mind is the only real antidote to worry, anxiety, fear, confusion, stress and frustration.

Meditation is a way of transforming your mind. By using techniques that encourage and promote concentration, positive feelings, clarity, a relaxed state, and a calm way of seeing the truth in all things, you can improve your mental and physical well being.

Meditation also offers an opportunity to get in touch with your mind on an intricate spiritual level in order to discover its habits and patterns. It is one of the most effective ways to cultivate new, positive and fulfilling ways of being.

Meditation exists beyond the mind

Meditation is a state of thoughtless awareness. It is not about effort or doing, rather it is simply a state of awareness.

According to Indian mystic, guru and spiritual teacher, Osho "All that the mind is capable of *doing* and *achieving* is not relevant when it comes to meditation – meditation is something beyond the mind. The mind is absolutely helpless when it comes to meditation."

Osho goes on to say that "The mind cannot penetrate meditation; where mind ends, meditation begins."

You and I have been taught to believe that everything can be done with the mind. So, when it comes to meditation, our natural inclination is to start thinking in terms of techniques, methods and what we can *do* to maximize our meditational experience.

It makes sense that we would think this way because so many things in life validate the use of the mind in getting what we want. We have been raised with the belief that "if you just put your mind to it, you can do anything." There is truth to that, yet the only thing that the mind cannot "do" is meditate.

Meditation techniques will teach you *how* to take control of and connect with your mind, but the necessity of that control only pertains to the degree in which it allows you to free yourself from your mind.

Meditation is your true nature. It is your being. It is fully you and it can only be entered into through the emptying of your mind. As Osho teaches "Meditation is not an achievement – it is something that already exists in you, it is your nature. It is there waiting for you – just turn inward and it is available. You have been carrying it always."

Meditation therefore is the simple process of removing your attention from current conditions and circumstances which when focused on too regularly fragment and cloud your perceptions.

When you allow for clear, unadulterated levels of conscious awareness to occur you access the spiritual being inside of you. This Spirit being is superior to your human mind and physical body and offers guidance and peace that you are unable to achieve at a human level.

As you consistently and patiently learn how to empty your mind, the deepened focus and concentration that you immerse yourself in will slowly create in you an intensely peaceful, powerful, clear and energised state of mind.

This spiritually energised state of mind is your intrinsic, Spirit nature that can guide and lead you in Truth and cause a transformative effect that will give you a new understanding of life.

Chapter 2

The History and Benefits of Meditation

The soul always knows what to do to heal itself. The challenge is to silence the mind.
- Caroline Myss

The History of Meditation

Meditation was barely recognized by Westerners until an Indian yoga teacher named Maharishi Mahesh Yogi introduced Transcendental Meditation (TM) to the United States in 1959. The meditation presented by Maharishi to Americans used a mantra that helped to stimulate relaxation and transcend conventional thinking.

The Beatles, who studied with Maharishi in India, were a big influence in the growing popularity of meditation through the 1960s. With his popularity, Maharishi continued to train more than forty thousand meditation teachers for the next fifty years. The teachers who trained directly under Maharishi then spread out and taught the transcendental meditation technique to more than five million people around the world.

During the last part of the 20th century, other methods of meditation began to gain recognition in the West. One of these new forms of meditation was called insight or mindfulness meditation.

Mindfulness meditation aims to help a person become deeply aware of the present moment in order to be able to completely live through the here and now.

Other forms of meditation utilize visualization and guided imagery through mental pictures to promote relaxation of both mind and body. Currently, over 20 million Americans, which comprise almost 10% of the population, perform regular meditation.

Their purpose for practicing meditation ranges from managing high blood pressure, stress, anxiety, and their overall state of mind in order to live better.

The Benefits of Meditation

As meditation increased in popularity over the years, more and more studies were conducted to explore the effects of meditation on the human mind and body. Scientists extensively researched the potential benefits of meditation and how it could help cure a wide range of physical, mental, emotional and even societal ailments.

Since its introduction in 1959, more than 600 research studies on meditation were carried out at 250 different universities and medical schools around the world to confirm the effectiveness of meditation.

The National Institutes of Health in the United States granted more than $24 million for research studies on the topic of meditation. These research studies are now recorded in more than 650 scientific and medical journals each of which provide proof of the benefits of meditation for medical conditions such as diabetes, cancer, chronic pain and heart disease.

Because of the deemed benefits of meditation, many businesses have started sponsoring meditation classes for their employees' well-being. This cost-effective solution enhances employee productivity and keeps employees happy.

Even public schools in the United States have started to teach meditation to both children and teenagers. A research study conducted by the Medical College of Georgia in 2003 discovered that meditation lowers stress and enhances interpersonal relationships between students. It was also discovered that it improves school performance.

The government has also started using meditation to lower crime rates and the US military uses meditation as an effective treatment for post-traumatic stress disorder acquired by soldiers sent out to war.

The Primary Benefits of Meditation

Meditation has been practiced in the East for several centuries though it is fairly new to the western world. Its benefits and ease of implementation has been easily recognized by western culture which has led to its rapid popularity growth.

For just a few minutes a day, with absolutely no cost or special equipment, anyone can take advantage of the benefits of meditation.

Despite its simplicity, the overall efficacy of meditation has made it the most valuable means for people to heal not only themselves but the planet as well.

A summary of the primary benefits of meditation:

Benefits for the body

Reduces inflammation – Stress leads to inflammation. Relaxation turns off the stress response therefore reducing the health risks caused by inflammation

Lowers high blood pressure by making the body less responsive to stress hormones

Decreases anxiety attacks by lowering the levels of blood lactate

Boosts the production of serotonin that improves mood and behavior

Reduces stress-related ailments including headaches, insomnia and ulcers

Boosts the immune system

Improves energy levels

Benefits for the mind

Creates emotional strength that helps fight against negative feelings of anger, tension and frustration

Improves creative inclinations

Boosts feelings of happiness

Helps put things into perspective. Problems that appeared big, begin to appear small

Expands intuition through improved clarity and peace of mind

Improves focus and concentration

Promotes calmness by not allowing any single negative thought to dominate the mind or body

Chapter 3

How Meditation Works

Meditation is all about the pursuit of nothingness. It's like the ultimate rest. It's better than the best sleep you've ever had. It's a quieting of the mind. It sharpens everything, especially your appreciation of your surroundings. It keeps life fresh.
- Hugh Jackman

The Mind, Body and Meditation

Why is meditation effective? When you meditate, you are able to focus entirely on the present moment because you cease from thinking about your personal worries, anxieties, work deadlines, and daily tasks.

During meditation, you are able to silence your mental clatter. This leads to a state of complete relaxation of not only your mind but your body as well.

The transformations experienced by the mind and body during meditation can be quantified scientifically. During the state of relaxation brought about by meditation both the heart rate and respiration are significantly slowed down. It has also been discovered that the frequency of the brain waves is decelerated during meditation.

When you are functioning at your normal level of consciousness your brain waves run at 13 to 30 cycles each second. This is dramatically reduced to 8 to 13 cycles per second during the meditative state.

It has also been found that during meditation the brain wave activity moves from the right frontal cortex to the left side. This finding is supported by renowned researcher and neuroscientist Richard J. Davidson, PhD at the University of Wisconsin.

Dr. Davidson has spent more than twenty years researching the positive effects of meditation. During one of his experiments, Dr. Davidson explored the brain activities of Buddhist monks to see how their regular meditation influenced their neural physiology.

He ascertained during that experiment that the Buddhist monks' left frontal cortex, which is the part of the brain connected to happiness, was more active compared to the left frontal cortex of people who do not meditate.

Research studies also show that meditation stimulates the body to release more endorphins, which are neurotransmitters known to induce positive feelings.

People who meditate regularly experience positive feelings more consistently than people who do not meditate regularly. They are therefore expected to live longer, happier and more productive lives.

Over the years, advanced brain-scanning equipment has helped scientists see the lasting physiological transformations brought about by meditation.

In a 2009 experiment, scientist Dr. Eileen Luders of UCLA proved that parts of the brain connected to concentration, focus and optimistic emotions were dramatically bigger in people who performed regular meditation as opposed to those that never meditated at all.

Dr. Jeffery Dusek of the Benson-Henry Institute for Mind Body Medicine in Massachusetts supported this by conducting a study that showed how regular meditation could create a positive alteration in cell metabolism.

The Healing Power of Meditation

The scientific research studies mentioned above (as well as hundreds of other studies) have convinced scientists and medical professionals of the positive effect of meditation in strengthening the areas of the brain connected to positive feelings. They have also proven that meditation has the ability to neutralize the harmful impact of depression, anxiety and stress.

This is the primary reason why a lot of doctors and medical professionals believe in the healing power of meditation. They both agree that many of the physical ailments humans experience are stimulated by tension and stress.

Dr. Charles L. Raison, the head of the Mind Body Program at Emory University School of Medicine in Atlanta, pointed out that "It's hard to think of an illness in which stress and mood don't figure." The calming and relaxing effect of meditation wards off many of these stress-induced ailments.

Studies have also shown that the brain wave alterations that result from regular meditation can stimulate production of stem cells which can help the human body renew and repair itself.

An experiment conducted by Dr. Doris Taylor, the head of the Center for Cardiovascular Repair at the University of Minnesota validated this fact.

The healing power of meditation is not only available to Buddhist monks and those that have been practicing meditation for a long time. It is also available to meditation newbie's as well.

Dr. Richard Davidson, head of the Lab for Affective Neuroscience at the University of Wisconsin-Madison concluded his research studies on this topic by saying "What we have found is that after a short time spent meditating, the act of meditation had profound effects, not only on how our subjects felt, but on their brain and body as well."

Chapter 4

Common Obstacles to Meditation

Meditation is painful in the beginning but it bestows immortal bliss and supreme joy in the end.
- Swami Sivananda

Despite the known benefits of meditation, many people still fail to practice meditation on a regular basis. The most common obstacles to meditation are:

Busyness / Not enough time

Claiming that you don't have enough time to meditate normally means that you haven't made it a high enough priority. If you are serious about making meditation part of your life, you need to make time for it. Here are some ways that you can do that.

Stop thinking that it has to take long

Remember that regular mediation, even if only practiced five minutes a day can have a strong, positive impact on both your inner and outer life. It will help make your energy clear and focused. When you function with clarity and focus your productivity and effectiveness will increase therefore enabling you to get more done in a day.

Meditation promotes meditation

Indian yogi and guru, Paramahansa Yogananda said "the more we meditate, the more we will want to meditate" Often it's just a matter of getting started. Once you begin, you will want to do it more and more.

Be creative in finding times and places to meditate

In amidst your daily activity take moments to stop, relax your mind and be mindful of the present moment. Start with short one minute moments and increase them from there.

If you have to wait for an appointment, or you are waiting in a grocery store line, take a moment to notice your breath and relax.

Mental chatter / Can't sit still

Sitting still sounds pretty simple but it can be quite tough. Right when you sit down to meditate you suddenly get hungry or thirsty, or you get an incessant itch that won't go away, or your mind starts running in circles thinking about what you need to get done, or who you have to call.

It is possible however to calm your mind and remain still and quiet. Some suggestions for doing that are:

Press through your unsettledness

Recognize that *learning* to sit still takes work. Understand that you have to *train* your body to remain calm and quiet.

Remember that it will pass

The more you practice meditation, the more you will be able to recognize your mental chatter, accept it and let it go. Eventually, you will get good at sitting still and being quiet. The peace, quiet and stillness that you experience during meditation will become something you look forward to.

Force your mind to focus

At first, you will have to force your mind to do what you want it to do. Before it is disciplined, your mind is like a badly behaved undisciplined child doing whatever it wants to do. It will rebel and resist the new habit you are teaching it.

Eventually your mind will behave and do what you tell it to do. Use practices like chanting, prayer and breathing exercises to focus your mind and bring it back to where you want it to be.

Falling asleep

You can be motivated to meditate yet fall asleep shortly after starting your meditation practice. This is normal at first however there are ways that you can combat this.

Choose an ideal time to meditate

The best time to meditate is fifteen minutes to half an hour after rising in the morning when you feel refreshed and wide awake. Mid-day meditation also works well. Try to avoid meditating just before bed.

Use your eyes

Paramahansa Yogananda suggested to "Squeeze your eyes shut several times, then open them wide and stare straight ahead. Repeat this practice once or twice more.

If you do this, sleepiness will cease to bother you." Keeping your eyes lifted during meditation helps you stay more alert and tuned into a higher level of consciousness.

Discouragement

To meditate successfully takes practice. No one expects to master the piano the first time they play it. It's the same with meditation. It takes time.

The Buddha said that stilling the mind is the most challenging yet rewarding task that we will ever undertake. The good news is that *every effort* toward inner calmness helps transform us over time.

Boredom

Modern society is full of knick knacks, gadgets and media that stimulate us on a daily basis. In amongst this playground of stimuli it's no wonder that meditation can seem boring.

Until you develop an appreciation for the beauty of inner silence you will just have to trust that getting to that place will be well worth the effort.

Not knowing how to meditate

We tend to make meditation more complicated than it is. Meditation is simply about being present in the moment. If you can sit down and breathe, you know how to meditate.

Simple mindfulness meditation has no goal other than sitting still, allowing yourself to be comfortable with just being, and calming your mind. Our culture has taught us to believe that there has to be a right and a wrong way of doing something.

Meditation doesn't adhere to this false belief. The fact that you sit down and calm your mind in your own personal way is enough.

Chapter 5

Types and Elements of Meditation

Buddha was asked, "What have you gained from meditation?" He replied, "Nothing! However, let me tell you what I lost: Anger, anxiety, depression, insecurity, fear of old age and death."

Meditation is a general term that pertains to the different ways in which a person can achieve a tranquil state of being. Following are some of the most popular types of meditation techniques that can support the goal of reducing stress, anxiety and depression and attaining inner peace.

Guided meditation

Guided meditation, also called guided imagery or visualization, is a form of meditation in which the individual is verbally guided into consciousness either by a live or recorded voice. The voice teaches the individual how to release tension, relax, concentrate on breathing by clearing the mind, and focus their attention.

Some guided meditations can last as long as 45 minutes and others as little as 5 minutes. Many guided meditations use tranquil background music to encourage a state of relaxation.

Guided meditation is used for releasing negative emotions, recalling past memories, and clarifying ones purpose. It is an intentional process of silencing the mind so that subconscious, spiritual thoughts can emerge.

To practice guided meditation, create a quiet, nurturing environment for yourself. Find a comfortable position, preferably sitting, and begin by slowly and deeply inhaling then exhaling. Do this at least five times. This will allow your body to start to slow down and relax into the meditation.

When your body feels as if it's entering a relaxed state, turn on the guided meditation on CD or MP3 and allow yourself to be guided.

Let your body relax while keeping your awareness on the voice that is guiding you. Focusing allows your body to achieve a deeper level of relaxation.

Guided meditation assists you in breathing slowly and deeply while relaxing and focusing your thoughts on a specific goal. It also helps you to open up to your higher purpose.

You can also perform a guided meditation as part of a class. There may be guided meditation classes available in your community that you can attend.

Mantra meditation

Transcendental Meditation is the most common type of mantra meditation. Its goal is to prevent distracting thoughts by the use of a mantra.

When practicing this type of meditation remain passive, and if thoughts other than your chosen mantra go through your mind, recognize the thoughts and then return to your mantra.

In this meditation technique, you will quietly and effortlessly say a calming word or phrase (not out loud) over and over as a way of focusing your mind and avoiding distractions.

Examples of words that you can choose to say are peace, still, calm, serene, silent, empty or any other word or phrase that is easy to remember or means something to you. It doesn't matter what word you choose. What matters most is that you repeat the word over and over.

Just let your mind whisper your mantra to yourself repeatedly. Stay focused on your chosen mantra and don't feel that you have to change it. If you notice your mind wandering, use your chosen word as an anchor and gently bring your mind back to focusing on the word.

Practice this technique for 10-20 minutes every day or at the least 3-4 times a week.

Do your best not to complicate this meditation. There is nothing else to do besides silently repeating your mantra to yourself.

Some other examples of mantras you can choose are:

I am beautiful

I love myself

I live a beautiful life

I am filled with love

I live an abundant life

I live in a state of peace and joy

You can also choose the simple sounds of the OM mantra to help you concentrate better. Consistent with Hinduism beliefs, the OM is an ancient sound that originated during the first creation.

To create the OM sound, follow these steps:

Say "ah"

Follow that with a long "o"

Then create an "mmmm" sound

Finish with a second or two of silence

Repeat from the start

You'll know that you are making the correct OM sound when you can feel the sound vibrating within your body.

Mindfulness meditation

The goal of this type of meditation is to use focused attention (on something physical like your breathing) to cultivate mental calmness. The goal of this meditation is to help you 'pay attention,' or be more 'mindful.' It helps you become aware of what is already true moment to moment.

Regular practice of this type of meditation enables you to become unconditionally present, and to objectively consider your thoughts and gain more self understanding.

In order to practice mindfulness meditation start by finding a quiet and comfortable place to sit. Make sure that your head, neck and back are straight but not stiff.

Try to focus on the present by putting aside all thoughts of the past or future. Focus on your breathing by being sensitive to the air moving in and out of your body. Pay particular attention to the way each breath is slightly different.

Acknowledge every thought that goes through your mind whether it involves fear, worry, hope, or anxiety. Don't suppress these thoughts when they happen, rather take note of them, remain calm and use your breathing as an anchor. Don't judge your thoughts, just recognize them and return to your breathing.

When your meditation time comes to a close, sit for a couple minutes, become aware of where you are and get up gradually.

Body scan meditation

Body scan meditation is a component of mindfulness meditation. Its purpose is to become aware of the different regions of your body and be sensitive to how each part feels.

True mind/body awareness doesn't judge the body or its aches and tensions rather it simply allows you to say 'hello' to your body with an awareness that enables you to release any tension, stress or illness that you may be harboring.

In order to practice body scan meditation begin by lying on the floor, on a mat, or your bed. Start with your left toes. Be sensitive to how they feel. Are they holding tension? Focus your exhales to this area of your body and direct your breathing deep into your toes. Next, move your attention to your heel, focusing your breath the same way to your left heel.

Repeat this same process with the arch, your calf, knee, thigh and then do the same thing with the right leg. After scanning your legs, concentrate your awareness and breath on your pelvis, then your lower back, abdomen, chest, shoulders, arms, hands, neck and head.

When you have finished scanning your individual body parts, unite them by focusing on how your fingers connect to your hands, which connect to your arms and so on. Be sensitive to sensations such as the feel of a blanket or body tingling. The objective is to see your body as a perfect whole, united by your breath that is flowing in and out of your body.

Candle meditation

Candle meditation is practiced by gazing at a candle flame. Many people enjoy this type of meditation because they find it easier to let go of thoughts when they are concentrating on something physical. This type of meditation is an excellent way to improve concentration skills and it can lead you into a deep, profound meditational experience.

In order to practice candle meditation you first need to place a candle in front of wherever you plan to sit for your meditation. Color has a great influence on us. It helps to balance and align us to the Universal Life Force. So, when you choose your candle be sensitive to its color. Below is a color chart that explains the powerful influence that color has on us.

When you are seated correctly and ready to meditate, simply stare at the candle and allow the image of the flame to occupy your mind. If distractions arise, gently lead your focus back to the candle.

Imagine that you are breathing the light of the candle in, then out. Do this by allowing your natural breathing rhythm to fill your awareness. Calmly sense that the light of the candle is flowing into you as you breathe in and out. Feel your body and mind being filled with purity and clarity as you do this.

In candle meditation your eyes are firmly fixed on the flame and because they are not moving your brain is not receiving any new information to process. As you continue to focus on the flame you notice that much of your peripheral vision begins to disappear. Eventually, you have no visual awareness but the flame and you enter deeper into your meditative experience.

After the completion of your candle meditation, remain seated or lie down. Close your eyes for at least five minutes and let your body and mind receive your experience on a conscious level.

Color Qualities from Historical and Metaphysical Views

White

Clarity, wholeness, purity, innocence and simplicity

Gold

Wealth, abundance, prosperity, spirituality and higher ideals

Silver

Accessing the subconscious mind, personal transformation

Violet

Connecting with the Divine, higher consciousness, reverence

Indigo

Intuition, wisdom, insight, clarity, imagination, clear thought

Blue

Self expression and communication, creativity, inspiration, trust

Turquoise

Healing, independence, protection

Green

Love, forgiveness, compassion, healing oneself, hope, freedom

Yellow

Self esteem, self respect, self discipline, ambition, inner power

Orange

Sensuality, sexual energy, happiness, optimism, friendship

Red

Survival, physical strength and vitality, safety, courage

Pink

Warmth, empathy, loyalty

Walking meditation

Not all meditation requires you to sit still during a session. Walking meditation for example, can be just as profound as a sitting meditation.

For a walking meditation the main object of meditation is your walking movements. The alternating left-right steps create a meditative state.

In order to perform a walking meditation set aside 20 minutes in which you can solely focus on your walking meditation. It is best not to combine it with trying to get somewhere, running errands or walking quickly for exercise.

Before starting, stand still and take some deep breaths. Put your full attention on breathing. At the same time, become aware of your body, how it feels standing and the sensations going on inside of it. Then allow your breathing to return to normal.

Next, begin walking at a slow but normal pace. Keep your attention focused on the sensations in your body as you walk. Notice how your feet feel connecting with the earth. Notice how your arms feel swaying at your sides. Also, take note of what your energy feels like inside your body.

You can even go further than this and scan all the parts of your body, the soles of your feet, your ankles, knees, chest, shoulders, fingertips, neck, face etc as you walk. If you feel tension anywhere, let it go by consciously relaxing that part of your body. When your mind wanders, don't worry, gently bring it back to the left-right-left motion of walking.

Walking a labyrinth can also be a very effective meditative practice. Before you begin, take a moment to transition from your daily life to the labyrinth experience. Stand still and breathe deeply then slowly return your breath to normal.

You can set an intention for the experience: questions, feelings, or affirmations, or you can simply just walk and see what the experience brings. The nice thing about a labyrinth is that it takes you out of your linear life experience. It mirrors the twists and turns in life and allows you to relax into them rather than resist them.

You can also set your focus on letting things go while you walk the labyrinth and then focus on what you will bring out from the center and back into your life.

Alternatively, you can use the same walking body scan as above while walking the labyrinth.

Prayer meditation

Unknown to many, prayer is a form of meditation that has been widely practiced for centuries all over the world. Meditative prayer involves meditation on scripture, devotional writing, a sunset, sunrise etc. Contemplative or listening prayer is the practice of emptying the mind, relaxing and being aware of the presence of God.

Meditative prayer involves silence, contemplation, stillness, and patience as you experience deeper meaning in what you read, or what you see etc.

Contemplative prayer is "the opening of the mind and heart – our entire being – to God, the Ultimate Mystery, beyond emotions, thoughts and words." It also involves silence, contemplation, stillness and patience.

In order to practice contemplative prayer it is important to choose a sacred word as a symbol of your intention to experience God's presence.

42

If your thoughts wander gently bring them back by repeating your sacred word.

Elements of Meditation

The different forms of meditation may employ different techniques but they share the following same elements:

Focused attention

Concentrated attention is the most vital component of meditation. When you focus your attention, you are able to set your mind free from day-to-day distractions that often cause tension and anxiety, and venture into a world of calmness, clarity and peace. What you focus on will vary depending on the type of meditation you are doing.

Peaceful breathing

To achieve relaxed, deep, even-paced breathing, it is important that you breathe using your diagram. Using your diaphragm is more efficient because it requires minimal action from your shoulders and neck muscles. The objective of slow and deep breathing is to bring more oxygen into your body. This calms you and creates an inner space that is conducive to meditation.

Quiet and comfortable setting

Advanced practitioners can perform meditation almost anywhere, even if the place is noisy or crowded. As a beginner, it is advisable for you to start practicing meditation in a quiet and comfortable place where you won't be distracted by others.

Before you start your meditation practice, get rid of any distractions. Turn off the television, radio and cell phone before you begin each session.

Chapter 6

How to Prepare for Meditation

Sometimes, simply by sitting, the soul collects wisdom
- Zen Proverb

Preparing for meditation is Stage Zero of the meditation process. With any kind of meditation it is important to do some preparation in order for things to go well.

Stage Zero is often seen as an optional extra, and either skipped or not done thoroughly. This is sad because it hinders the effectiveness of ones meditation even before it begins.

If you want to get a certain result, you need to set up the right conditions to get that result. According to Buddhists, there is a principle called "conditionality" which states that if your goal is to achieve "x," you need to set up the conditions that will enable you to achieve "x."

Buddhists put a heavy emphasis on the importance of preparation. They believe that it's impossible to skip this step and expect to get the results that you desire.

Preparing for meditation involves both the external and internal. Externally you want to prepare a place that will be conducive to a deep, meditative experience. Internally, you want to address your posture, deepen your awareness of your body, and relax as deeply as you can. This preparation is essential for a calmer, less stressed and more peaceful mind.

Following are some suggestions on how you can prepare your external and internal environment in a way that will help you get the most out of your meditation.

Mirror your internal intention by an external act

Mentally you are unloading your mind of all irrelevant, powerless human thoughts in order to reload it with thoughts that are in line with your spiritual higher self.

Physically, you can express your intent to purify your thoughts by taking a shower (to wash away your troubles), brushing your teeth, or washing your hands and face. The act of washing yourself is a very symbolic cleansing ritual that will make you feel renewed, refreshed and clean. It can also have an extremely positive effect on your mood and overall mindset as you prepare to meditate.

Create a relaxing atmosphere

If you want your body and mind to relax then create an atmosphere that is conducive to relaxation.

Light a candle, burn some incense, dim the lights, place some fresh flowers on the table, or play some meditation music. Creating a sanctuary in which to meditate will go a long way in helping you clear your mind and experience a deep, enjoyable and enriching meditation.

Provoke a meditative state

Take 5-20 minutes to read spiritual writings. These can vary between spiritual God-centered writings, spiritual healing material or even some positive encouraging words that feed your soul and get you in touch with Spirit. As you read, absorb and reflect on the meaning of every sentence. Take notes in a special journal that you exclusively reserve for spiritual reflection.

Breathe deep

When you feel that your spiritual reading has led you to a state of awareness and peace, take between 5-10 slow, deep breaths. As you breathe inward open yourself to the peaceful, loving nature of God (or Universe). Let your outward breath release your tension and frustrations that are held within your unconscious. Let them go. Now begin the meditation practice of your choice. Breathe from your diaphragm and feel your body relaxing with every full, deep breath.

Choose the best time for you

There are no set rules in terms of the ideal time to meditate. It will depend on what works best for you and your schedule.

Morning meditation is preferred by some people because it helps set a good mood for the rest of the day. Others prefer meditating after work or school because it helps them let go of the tensions of the day.

There are still others who opt to meditate right before bed in order to allow their unconscious minds to work on their intentions while they sleep. Some people will find this time difficult because they are tired and have to fight their desire to fall asleep.

Choose the time of day that suits you best. This might involve some trial and error but once you find your ideal time it will nurture your meditative practice for months or even years to come.

Get comfortable and sit correctly

First, choose comfortable clothes that will not restrict or confine you. Make sure that the area you have designated as your meditation sanctuary is warm.

The way you sit during meditation is extremely important. Why? Because the emotions and mental state that you experience during meditation are ultimately attributed to the way you hold your body. Even something as intricate as the angle at which you hold your chin can affect how much thinking you do.

So one of the first things you need to learn is how to sit properly. There are two vitally important principles you need to remember in setting up a suitable posture for meditation:

*Your posture has to allow you to be comfortable and relaxed

*Your posture has to allow you to be alert and aware

If you are uncomfortable, you won't be able to meditate. If you can't relax you won't be able to enjoy your meditation.

You might consider sitting cross-legged on a meditation pillow. However, if you are not very flexible, you will probably suffer doing this. Your best bet is to sit in a chair that you find comfortable and that allows you to sit upright. Here are some elements of good posture that you should consider when sitting.

Your spine should be relaxed and upright. Avoid slouching. Your shoulders should be relaxed and rolled back and down a little bit. Your hands should be supported either on your lap, on the arms of a chair or resting on a cushion.

Your head should be balanced with your chin tucked in slightly and the back of your neck should feel long and relaxed. Your face should be relaxed and contain no tension anywhere. Have your feet flat on the floor.

There are specialist meditation chairs available to help you sit comfortably and achieve an optimum posture. You can search "meditation chairs" online to see what's available.

Avoid meditating right after a big meal

Research studies show that mind activity is intensified when the body is metabolizing food. To avoid unnecessary noise in your head, choose not to do your meditation right after a big meal.

Don't rush off after meditation

After completing your meditation, sit quietly for a little while longer. Use this time to assimilate your experience, as well as reflect and contemplate on it. Be conscious of the intuition or revelation that you might be feeling.

Doing this enables you to fully embrace your meditative experience. It also acts as a gateway for allowing the experience to become part of your 'real world' rather than keeping it as something separate from your day to day life. As you learn to listen to your inner voice, your 'real self' will begin to guide you on a daily basis.

Make meditation a daily habit

The benefits you will gain from meditation are cumulative. This means that as you continue to regularly meditate, you will acquire more and more benefits.

If you are truly serious about improving yourself through meditation, make it a part of your daily routine by meditating at least once or twice per day. The rewards you gain will improve with commitment and regularity.

Chapter 7

How to Practice Meditation Every Day

Practice meditation regularly. Meditation leads to eternal bliss. Therefore meditate, meditate.
- Swami Sivananda

Consider meditation the most important activity in your day

A most helpful approach to your daily meditation practice is to consider it the most important activity in your day. Schedule it into your day just as you would an extremely important appointment, then do everything you can to keep your appointment.

The reason most people struggle with a daily meditation practice is because they don't realize how integral to daily life those 20-30 minutes of focused time are. Either you are going to function through the day with a clear mind energized by Spirit energy or you are going to stumble through the day powered by nothing but clunky human energy and a cluttered mind.

Meditation allows you to access your spiritual, more superior self that functions with effortlessness and clarity. Things that seem overwhelming to the human mind are put into perspective by the spiritual mind.

So, meditation actually saves you time. At first, as a beginner it can appear to take a lot of time, but when you understand that it brings clarity to everything you experience in a day, you will be more apt to do it regularly in order to function effectively every day.

Start small

Don't fall into the trap of overdoing it in the beginning. If you jump into meditation expecting to do 20-30 solid minutes of focused meditation daily, you'll be quickly disappointed with your results.

You will find that mastering even 5 minutes of meditation at the beginning will be hard enough.

Remember that you are forming a new habit and with any new habit there is a period of pain before it becomes a regular practice in your life. So, try to avoid overinflated efforts at the beginning.

Start with something you know you can manage. Aim at getting 3-5 minutes of focused, sitting still time in each day for one week. Most beginners find that this is a manageable way to develop their meditation practice.

If you are successful at doing that keep adding 3-5 minutes until you get yourself up to regularly meditating for 20-30 minutes a day. If you have trouble even getting 5 minutes of solid meditation time a day, you need to step back and take an honest look at what's really holding you back from making meditation a part of your daily life.

Track your practice

If you have a tough time being accountable to yourself, try tracking your meditation practice. When you do this, your calendar becomes your accountability pal because you make yourself responsible for marking an "X" on every day that you meditate.

Put your calendar in a place where you can look at it every day. Ideally, marking an "X" on the calendar for every day that you meditate should be motivating for you. If the "X" doesn't motivate you, try a cute sticker or some symbol that inspires you.

Journal

It can also be motivating to keep a journal of your meditative experiences. Writing down what you learned or experienced can be something that you look forward to after your meditation practice. If you are a personal growth seeker you will find that looking back on your journal entries can teach you a lot about your own inner journey.

Use your time wisely

How much TV does the average American watch in a day? The answer: 4-5 hours. If you are considering making meditation a regular part of your life then you must be the type of person that seeks to have a more fulfilling life experience.

Weigh the pros and cons of watching excessive amounts of television. Does watching television benefit your life in a positive way? Does it enable you to be the person you want to be? If your answer is no, consider minimizing your TV viewing time. Replace that time with an activity that will benefit your future, namely, meditation.

Meditate with a group

Consider meditating with a group on a regular basis. Scout out meditation groups or meditation classes in your community. Being part of a group can give you a feeling of comradery. You might also find it motivational to develop relationships with other people that are interested in enriching their lives through meditation.

Hire a meditation coach

If you find it hard motivating yourself to meditate you can hire a mindfulness coach that can help you uncover any unconscious principles that might be holding you back from meditating on a regular basis.

A meditation coach can also assist you with making the most of your meditative time and helping you overcome the common difficulties with meditation. They can also act as an accountability partner for you.

Avoid judging your meditation

Be easy on yourself. Meditation is never about thinking you have to be *good* at it. There is no good or bad when it comes to meditation. Meditation just "is." It isn't anything more than that. You just need to learn to let it be whatever it is because whatever it is will still be to your benefit.

If you understand the long term purpose of your meditative practice this won't be a problem.

Find a meditation buddy

Find a friend who is also trying to develop a meditation practice. You don't have to meditate in the same place or at the same time. You just need to be there to keep each other accountable and encourage each other.

Commit for the long term

There is something about commitment that enables you to remain accountable to your goal. Commit yourself to a daily meditation practice for one month. Break that goal down into achievable weekly goals. Then break that down further into achievable daily goals.

Schedule a time for your meditation. Research has proven that scheduling a specific time to do something makes you eight times more likely to do it.

After you've scheduled your meditation into your day, try your best to live in day tight compartments. Don't look at your one month goal and wonder how you'll ever get there. Instead focus on what you need to do that day.

Create a routine

Think "same time, same place." This will help you stay steady in turning your new practice into a fully functioning habit.

Relate your daily meditation practice to a habit

Think of another fully established habit you already have working in your life. Pair your meditation practice with that habit. For example, think "go to the gym then meditate" or "meditate, then tea." This enables you to start making meditation part of your daily routine.

Be flexible

Make sure to be flexible with your routine. Something unexpected can interrupt your daily meditation practice. When this happens realize that not every day will look the same. Simply switch your meditation to a different time.

Don't use this as an excuse to exclude mediation from your day.

Consider the benefits

After each session, take a moment to consider how you feel and what you gained from your meditation. The sooner you begin to see the benefits, the sooner you will find it easier to maintain a consistent practice.

Keep your expectations in check

Daily meditation takes time to develop. Learning how to sit still can be a challenge in itself for the beginner. You might see some immediate results or it might take longer. Remember that developing a regular meditation practice is a life-long skill, not a quick fix.

Know why you are meditating

Usually, maintaining a daily meditation practice is more about the "why" than anything else. Always remind yourself *why* you are meditating. If you ever find yourself slipping, bring yourself back to your "why." Write it down if you have to and review it in order to renew your commitment to it.

Use guided instruction

As a beginner, it is recommended that you follow a guided meditation for several weeks in order to get familiar with the meditative process. Over time you can choose to do whatever type of meditation works best for you.

Some recommended teachers who offer guided meditation CD's and MP3's are Louise Hay, Deepak Chopra, Stephen Levine, Jon Kabat Zinn, Sharon Salzberg and Jack Kornfield.

Keep it fresh

Feel free to keep things fresh by incorporating a variety of meditation techniques into your life. If you prefer however to use one method that works well for you, do that.

Meditation is entirely personal so what works for one person won't necessarily work for another person. When you take the time to formulate a meditative practice that works well for you it will benefit your life in numerous ways for years to come.

Conclusion

Congratulations on finishing the book!

I'm passionate about meditation and have made every effort to help you understand how to meditate so that you too can experience the transformational benefits that it has to offer.

I hope this book gave you all the necessary information you needed to understand meditation better and apply it to your life in order to reduce stress and anxiety and achieve unending success.

I know first-hand how powerful meditation is and I'm glad that you gave me the opportunity to share its many benefits with you.

Thank you again for purchasing this book. I sincerely hope this information changes your life for the better.

Preview of
Mindfulness for Beginners

How to Live in the Moment, Stress and Worry Free in a Constant State of Peace and Happiness

Available on Amazon

Chapter 1

What is Mindfulness?

"Mindfulness means paying attention in a particular way: on purpose, in the present moment, and non-judgmentally. This kind of attention nurtures greater awareness, clarity and acceptance of present-moment reality."
Dr. Jon Kabat-Zinn

The History and Definition of Mindfulness

Buddhism referenced the concept of mindfulness over 2500 years ago. The word "mindfulness" comes from the Pali language which was indigenous to the Indian subcontinent.

The word "mindfulness" is a combination of the Pali words "Sati" and "Sampajana." These two words when put together translate to mean awareness, discernment, circumspection and retention.

Linguistic scholars that studied these terms defined mindfulness as *remembering to have a caring and discerning moment-to-moment awareness of what is happening in ones immediate reality.*

When the concept of mindfulness was first introduced to Western science it was thought that mindfulness, along with the meditation practices it encourages was connected to religious beliefs and therefore only attainable by a select group of people.

Several decades later these myths were dispelled and Western science came to understand mindfulness as an inbred aspect of human consciousness. That is, an inherent ability to be aware of the present moment.

The most common Western definition of mindfulness is by Dr. Jon Kabat-Zinn, one of the main founders of the field of mindfulness. His definition of mindfulness is "paying attention in a particular way: on purpose, in the present moment, and non-judgmentally."

Mindfulness can also be understood by contrasting the word with its opposite, *mindlessness*. Mindlessness is when awareness and attention is scattered and unfocused due to a preoccupation with worry, the past, or the future. Mindlessness causes limited attention and awareness to what's going on in the present moment thus depleting ones power to live the present day to the fullest.

Understanding Mindfulness

We live in a busy world. Men and women everywhere are up at the crack of dawn rushing through breakfast, chatting on the phone and answering emails .Families are stuck on a 24/7 merry-go-round of work, school, after school activities, appointments etc.

When the day finally winds down, most people zone out in front of the television for some much needed down time.

Yet days come and go and the rush of accomplishing an endless list of "to-do's" often leaves people lacking a connection with the present moment – missing out on the special moments that lie within what they are doing.

Living on "automatic pilot" becomes the norm for most people. Sure they're alive but they're not really living each moment. It's kind of like sleepwalking. They go through the motions but somehow seem absent from their own life.

On automatic pilot the brain becomes a plethora of thoughts that skip from one unfinished idea to another. Each thought rudely and obnoxiously interrupts another with a jumble of questions, answers, pondering and arguing all of which are overlapped with endless pictures, ideas, desires and memories.

Mindfulness is a way of reconnecting with life itself. It is a form of self-awareness that allows one to take a step back from the noise of the mind and observe the mental activity and the feelings it generates. By doing this it is possible to separate oneself from the influence of an overactive, 'on automatic pilot' mind.

The Key Ingredients of Mindfulness

Freedom from the chaos of mental activity

Freedom to live in the present moment

Freedom from judgment

Freedom from attachment

Freedom from the chaos of mental activity

Mindfulness enables you to be an "observer" of your thoughts and feelings rather than a victim of them. The chaos of mental activity has no purpose other than to make you a prisoner of its perpetual circle of craziness.

When you learn to be mindful, you learn how to relax and act as a witness of your inner life. You become free from the negative effects of mental chaos and free from judging yourself, others and the world at large.

As you begin to master "observation," you begin to live in the moment and not on autopilot. The more you do this, the more you come to experience relaxation, stillness and a sense of freedom.

Freedom to live in the present moment

Freedom to live in the present moment simply means that you apply the fullness of your conscious awareness to each moment. Freely experiencing each moment stops you from dividing your conscious awareness between today and yesterday as well as today and tomorrow.

Buddha himself said "The secret of health for both mind and body is not to mourn for the past, worry about the future, or anticipate troubles, but to live in the present moment wisely and earnestly."

Freedom from judgment

Being free from judgment simply means that you do not attach your opinions to the happenings of the present moment but rather act as an independent observer without disturbing them by your preferences and prejudices.

Opinions, preferences and prejudices are based on judgments using criteria from past experiences. They are thus stale and therefore cannot be applied to the freshness of the present moment.

When you are mindful, you consciously stay alert and attentive to each moment. Instead of judging things as "good" or "bad" you simply acknowledge and accept them without judgment. This enables you to be freed from reacting to the events and circumstances around you that are often beyond your control.

When you live on autopilot, your reactions, thoughts and feelings just happen to you without you having any say in the matter. When you are attentive and mindful of the present moment, you respond to things with acceptance and openness.

Mindfulness allows you to choose how you will react to events and experiences in your life. If you choose to judge an event, even though mindfulness teaches you not to judge, then your judgment of the event will only be useless and harmful to you.

For example, if your judgment of an event causes you to boil over with anger, then all you have done is boil over with anger. The fact that you're angry is useless. It doesn't change the situation and neither does it benefit the situation. All it does is cause you bodily harm because it creates stress.

Buddha said "You will not be punished for your anger; you will be punished *by* your anger."

When you choose to remain free from judgment, you accept things as they are. You look at "what is" and accept it as such.

Living life free from judgment allows you to control your state of mind in every moment and in every situation.

Freedom from attachment

It is easy to remain attached to old views and wrong perceptions that you've had for a long time. This type of narrow-mindedness forces negative, useless perceptions and opinions onto the events of the present moment.

Attachment is closely related to judgment because it is a personal opinion that you use to assess the happenings of the moment. In order to live in a state of mindfulness, it is important to let go of old views and wrong perceptions in order to remain an observer and one that accepts things as they are without opinion.

The Key Benefits of Mindfulness

Mindfulness has unlimited benefits that cut across all spheres of life. The overall key benefits of mindfulness are:

It heightens your level of awareness

It enables you to fully experience the present moment

It allows you to distinguish between the real you and your thoughts

It eliminates stress by making you an observer of your thoughts rather than someone that is constantly entangled by them

It supports attitudes that promote a satisfying life

It enables you to become more connected and in harmony with your being, the nature of human beings and the nature of things

It allows you to develop self-acceptance which yields self-contentment and compassion

It enables you to be fully engaged in day to day activities

It helps you enjoy life as it happens

It gives you a greater ability to deal with adverse situations

It increases your concentration and focus

It enables you to see that life is dynamic and that things change. Hence thoughts and feelings come and go

It gives you the freedom to experience calmness and peacefulness despite whatever is going on around you

It creates more balance in your emotions and reactions thus enabling you to be free from the chaos of emotional spikes and outbursts

It increases your awareness of the habits you've created in your thoughts and feelings.

It enables you to see thoughts as thoughts and feelings as feelings. This prevents you from getting caught up in them

It makes it more likely that you will make wise choices rather than ones based on stressful thought patterns that are fueled by confusion.

It allows you to remain free from the worries of the future and the regrets of the past

It allows you to maintain successful relationships because you develop the skill of communicating your emotions in a calm, professional way

It promotes self-insight, intuition, morality and fear modulation

Mindfulness improves physical health by:

Lowering blood pressure

Reducing chronic pain

Improving sleep

Relieving stress and worry

Alleviating gastrointestinal difficulties

Mindfulness can help treat:

Anxiety

Depression

Eating disorders (compulsive overeating, bulimia, anorexia)

Substance abuse

Obsessive-compulsive disorder

Available on Amazon

About the Author

"A stress free, healthy and positive life is available to anyone that is willing to change."

Living a life of peace, great health and happiness shouldn't feel like something that is available to everyone but you. There is a whole world of limitless possibility out there but only YOU can make it a reality in your own life.

My name is Yesenia Chavan. I use to be stressed-out, overweight, unhappy and desperate to live the 'great life' I dreamed of. There were many years that I lived as a victim of circumstance completely oblivious to the fact that I had the power to choose the kind of life I wanted to live.

One day, completely stressed-out by my situation, I made a decision to learn everything I could on inner peace, happiness and taking control of my life. I devoured every book I could get my hands on and eagerly applied everything I learned to my life.

Slowly I started experiencing more peace, health and happiness than I ever had before. For the first time in my life I felt that I was in complete control of my destiny. Life became an exciting, rich, beautiful playground that I couldn't wait to enjoy every day. Positive things started happening for me. I hit my goal weight, started living my passion and tripled my income. It still amazes me today how one quality decision could transform my life so drastically.

Now I'm on a mission to share what I've learned in a straight-forward, simple, to-the-point kind of way that will enable you to transform your life in a short amount of time.

You're busy and the last thing you need is to wade through a 500 page book on how to find peace, release stress, get healthy and live happy. That's why my books are concise, easy to read and aim to answer your most pressing questions.

Everything I write comes from the heart and my goal with every book is to help you live the stress free, happy life you were meant to live.

When I'm not writing I enjoy yoga, long walks, spending time at the beach and reading.

Thank you for exploring my books. My hope is that they will be a light for you as so many books were to me.

Made in the USA
San Bernardino, CA
05 September 2015